Thank you...

...for purchasing this copy of Get Ready for Year 2.

We hope that you will find the book helpful in preparing your child to move up to their next year-group. You may choose to use it during the final few months of Year 1, during the summer holidays or in the first few months of Year 2.

On our Teachers and Parents pages we summarise the likely content of each subject in Year 2. On the children's pages we feature activities that will help prepare children for most of their subjects, hopefully giving them confidence to take part in their lessons with enthusiasm, skills and knowledge.

This book is part of our growing range of educational titles. Most of our books are individual workbooks but, due to popular demand, we are now introducing a greater number of photocopiable titles especially for teachers.

To find details of our other publications, please visit our website:

www.acblack.com

CONTENTS

Numeracy	Information for Adults	Page 3
	Activities	Pages 4 - 15
Literacy	Information for Adults	Page 16
	Activities	Pages 17 - 28

Science
Design Technology
Information Technology

	Information for Adults	Page 29
	Activities	Pages 30 - 34

Religious Education
Art
Geography
History
Music
Physical Education

	Information for Adults	Page 35
	Activities	Pages 36 - 40

The National Curriculum shows that every child in Year 2 needs to be taught mathematics. How the maths is to be taught is shown in the National Numeracy Strategy. The following aspects of maths will be included during the Numeracy Hour which takes place each day in Year 2:

- ✓ Reading and writing numbers to at least 100.
- ✓ Counting to at least 100.
- ✓ Putting Numbers in order of size.
- ✓ Using simple number sequences, odd numbers and even numbers for example.
- ✓ Understanding that subtraction is the inverse of addition.
- ✓ Addition facts for numbers up to at least 10.
- ✓ Subtraction facts for numbers up to at least 10.
- ✓ Multiplying as a form of repeated addition.
- ✓ Learning the 2 and 10 times tables and using these to work out simple divisions.
- ✓ Beginning to learn the 5 times table.
- ✓ Using halving and doubling.
- ✓ Solving problems by calculating efficiently.
- ✓ Telling the time: o'clock, half past, quarter to and quarter past.
- ✓ Estimating and measuring lengths.
- ✓ Reading scales, e.g. using a ruler to the nearest centimetre, reading bathroom or kitchen scales, reading levels on thermometers or measuring jugs.
- ✓ Using the correct names for shapes.
- ✓ Using vocabulary such as clockwise and anticlockwise to describe positions and directions.
- ✓ Beginning to identify right angles.

On the next 12 pages we provide activities to strengthen children's abilities in handling numbers and to introduce some of the prerequisites for learning the aspects of maths listed above.

ODDS AND EVENS

These are called odd numbers.
↓ ↓ ↓ ↓ ↓
1 2 3 4 5 6 7 8 9 10
   ↑   ↑   ↑   ↑   ↑
These are called even numbers.

Copy out the odd numbers:

☐ ☐ ☐ ☐ ☐

Copy out the even numbers:

☐ ☐ ☐ ☐ ☐

Shade the odd numbers blue.   These are odd too.
                                                 ↓   ↓   ↓
| 1 | 2 | 3 | 4 | 5 | 6 | 7 | 8 | 9 | 10 | 11 | 12 | 13 | 14 | 15 |

Shade the even numbers red.   ↑   ↑
                                                  These are even too.

Does your house have a number?

If it does, is it an odd number or an even number?

Write the missing numbers:

| 22 | | 24 | | 26 | | 28 | | 30 | | 32 | | 34 | | 36 | |

Write the missing numbers:

| | 45 | | 47 | | 49 | | 51 | | 53 | | 55 | | 57 | |

Look carefully, then write the missing numbers:

| 18 | | 16 | | 14 | | 12 | | 10 | | 8 |

ADDITION AND SUBTRACTION

 Three add four makes seven.

 Seven subtract four makes three.

3 + 4 = 7 ⟶ 7 − 4 = 3

Try these:

5 + 1 = ☐ ⟶ ☐ − 5 = 1

6 + 2 = ☐ ⟶ ☐ − 6 = 2

7 + 3 = ☐ ⟶ ☐ − 7 = 3

3 + 2 = ☐ ⟶ ☐ − 3 = 2

4 + 2 = ☐ ⟶ ☐ − 4 = 2

8 + 5 = ☐ ⟶ ☐ − 8 = 5

6 + 6 = ☐ ⟶ ☐ − 6 = 6

9 + 7 = ☐ ⟶ ☐ − 9 = 7

10 + 10 = ☐ ⟶ ☐ − 10 = 10

CLOCKS

Write the missing numbers on the clock.

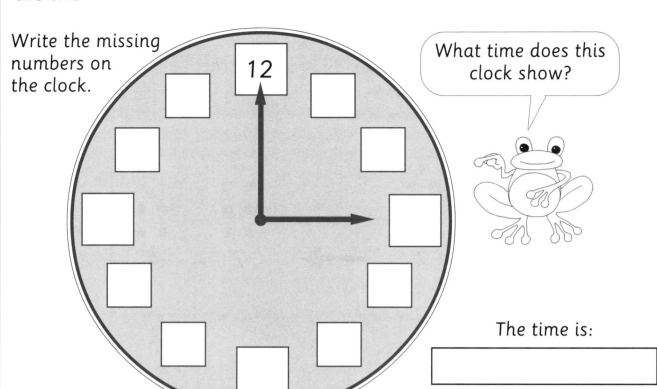

What time does this clock show?

The time is:

Practise the spellings:

1	one	
2	two	
3	three	
4	four	
5	five	
6	six	
7	seven	
8	eight	
9	nine	
10	ten	
11	eleven	
12	twelve	

clock	
o'clock	
half past	
hour	
minute	
second	
day	
night	
midnight	

WHAT TIME IS IT?

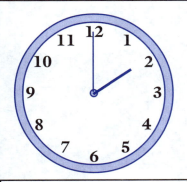  

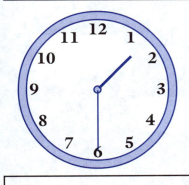 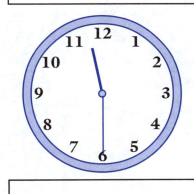 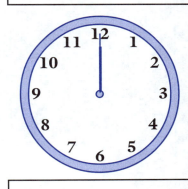

Both of these clocks say half past four.

This is an *analogue* clock.

This is a *digital* clock.

ADDITION STARS
Complete the addition stars. We have done some for you.

ADDITION STARS

Complete the addition stars. We have done some for you.

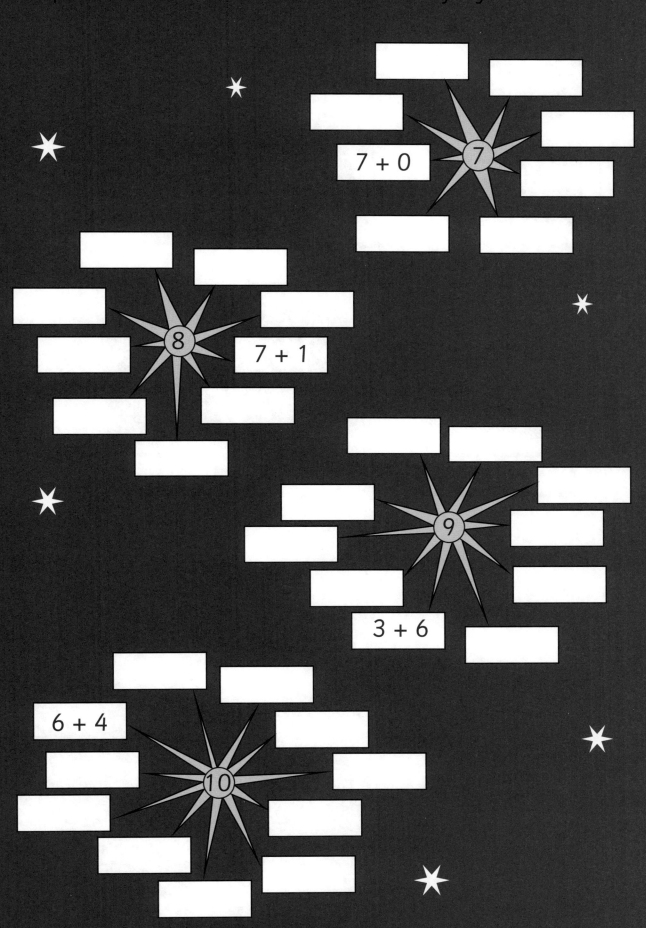

SHAPES

Write the correct names for the shapes using these words:

circle   triangle   square   rectangle   star

 A pentagon has five sides.

An octagon has eight sides.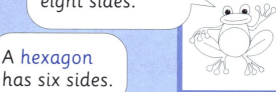

A hexagon has six sides.

Write the correct names for the shapes below.

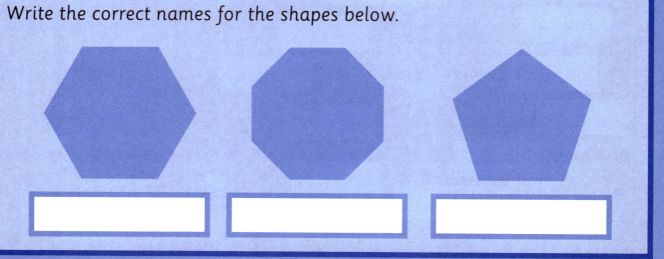

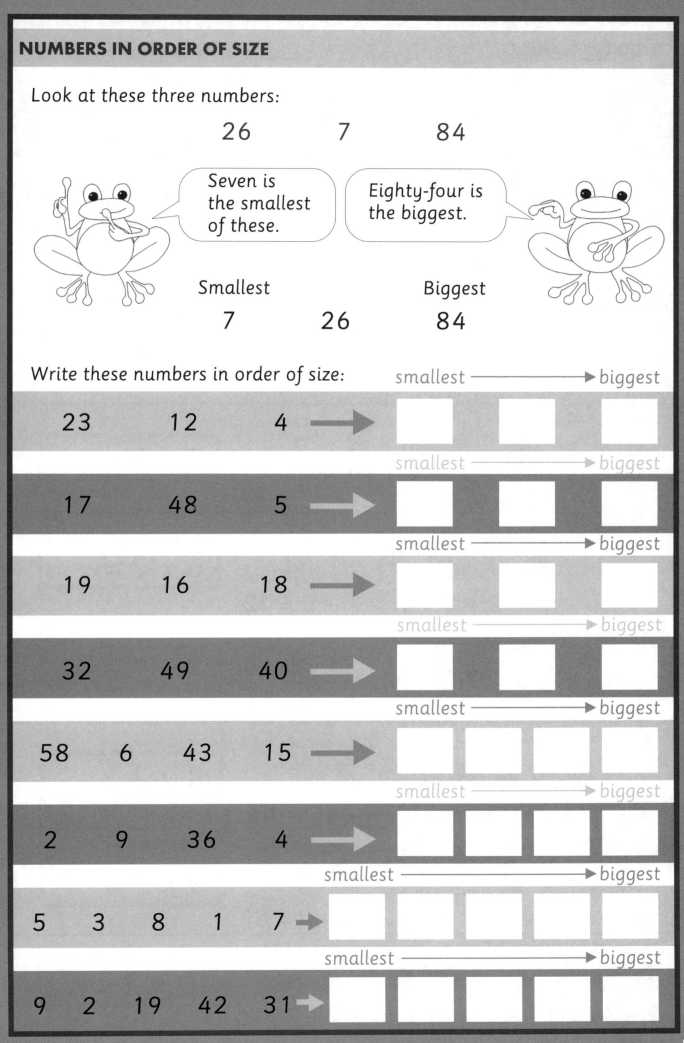

THE 2 TIMES TABLE

 Here is one pair of socks. 2 socks

1 x 2 = 2

Two pairs of socks.

2 x 2 =

Three pairs of socks.

3 x 2 =

Four pairs of socks.
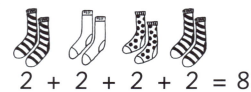
2 + 2 + 2 + 2 = 8

4 x 2 =

Five pairs of socks.

2 + 2 + 2 + 2 + 2 = 10

5 x 2 =

Six pairs of socks.

2 + 2 + 2 + 2 + 2 + 2 = 12

6 x 2 =

Seven pairs of socks.

2 + 2 + 2 + 2 + 2 + 2 + 2 = 14

7 x 2 =

Eight pairs of socks.

2 + 2 + 2 + 2 + 2 + 2 + 2 + 2 = 16

8 x 2 =

Nine pairs of socks.

2 + 2 + 2 + 2 + 2 + 2 + 2 + 2 + 2 = 18

9 x 2 =

Ten pairs of socks.

2 + 2 + 2 + 2 + 2 + 2 + 2 + 2 + 2 + 2 = 20

10 x 2 =

THE 10 TIMES TABLE

 Here is a pair of footprints. There are 10 toes. 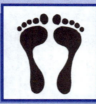 1 x 10 = 10

Here are 20 toes. + 10 = 20

2 x 10 = 20

Here are 30 toes. + 10 + 10 = 30

3 x 10 =

Here are ☐ toes.
10 + 10 + 10 + 10 = 40

4 x 10 =

Here are ☐ toes.
10 + 10 + 10 + 10 + 10 = 50

5 x 10 =

Here are ☐ toes.
10 + 10 + 10 + 10 + 10 + 10 = 60

6 x 10 =

Here are ☐ toes.
10 + 10 + 10 + 10 + 10 + 10 + 10 = 70

7 x 10 =

Here are ☐ toes.
10 + 10 + 10 + 10 + 10 + 10 + 10 + 10 = 80

8 x 10 =

Here are 90 toes.
10 + 10 + 10 + 10 + 10 + 10 + 10 + 10 + 10 = 90

9 x 10 =

Here are 100 toes.
10 + 10 + 10 + 10 + 10 + 10 + 10 + 10 + 10 + 10 = 100

10 x 10 =

THE 5 TIMES TABLE

 Here is a hand

There are 5 fingers

$1 \times 5 = 5$

Here are 10 fingers. $\boxed{5} + \boxed{5} = \boxed{10}$

$2 \times 5 = 10$

Here are 15 fingers. $\boxed{5} + \boxed{5} + \boxed{5} = \boxed{15}$

$3 \times 5 =$

Here are ☐ fingers.
$5 + 5 + 5 + 5 = 20$

$4 \times 5 =$

Here are ☐ fingers.
$5 + 5 + 5 + 5 + 5 = 25$

$5 \times 5 =$

Here are ☐ fingers.
$5 + 5 + 5 + 5 + 5 + 5 = 30$

$6 \times 5 =$

Here are ☐ fingers.
$5 + 5 + 5 + 5 + 5 + 5 + 5 = 35$

$7 \times 5 =$

Here are ☐ fingers.
$5 + 5 + 5 + 5 + 5 + 5 + 5 + 5 = 40$

$8 \times 5 =$

Here are 45 fingers.
$5 + 5 + 5 + 5 + 5 + 5 + 5 + 5 + 5 = 45$

$9 \times 5 =$

Here are 50 fingers.
$5 + 5 + 5 + 5 + 5 + 5 + 5 + 5 + 5 + 5 = 50$

$10 \times 5 =$

TIMES TABLE PRACTICE

Practise the times tables you have learnt.

1 x 2 =	1 x 5 =	1 x 10 =
2 x 2 =	2 x 5 =	2 x 10 =
3 x 2 =	3 x 5 =	3 x 10 =
4 x 2 =	4 x 5 =	4 x 10 =
5 x 2 =	5 x 5 =	5 x 10 =
6 x 2 =	6 x 5 =	6 x 10 =
7 x 2 =	7 x 5 =	7 x 10 =
8 x 2 =	8 x 5 =	8 x 10 =
9 x 2 =	9 x 5 =	9 x 10 =
10 x 2 =	10 x 5 =	10 x 10 =

 Double three makes six.

Half of six is three.

Doubles and halves:

Double 3	=	2 x 3	=		Half of 6 =	
Double 5	=	2 x 5	=		Half of 10 =	
Double 7	=	2 x 7	=		Half of 14 =	
Double 6	=	2 x 6	=		Half of 12 =	
Double 10	=	2 x 10	=		Half of 20 =	

During their literacy work in Year Two, your children will build on the work they have done in Year One. They will experience the daily Literacy Hour, in which they will read books guided by their teachers and they will learn about aspects of grammar, spelling and writing. The lessons will include work on:

- ✓ Beginning to form joined handwriting.

- ✓ Words with common letter patterns, including ch ph and wh.

- ✓ Using their growing awareness of grammar and context, to read unfamiliar words and to make predictions from a text

- ✓ Use of capital letters in appropriate places.

- ✓ Collecting favourite poems, and beginning to appreciate aspects including presentation, rhyme, rhythm and alliteration.

- ✓ The differences between written and spoken language.

- ✓ The language of time, with use of words such as after, then, meanwhile, etc.

- ✓ Writing simple instructions.

- ✓ Recognising syllables in polysyllabic words.

- ✓ Common prefixes and suffixes.

- ✓ The need for grammatical agreement, e.g. I am; they are.

- ✓ Identification and understanding of speech marks.

- ✓ The use of simple sentences in their own writing.

- ✓ Understanding alphabetical order, and the use of dictionaries to locate words by their initial letter.

- ✓ The use of commas in lists.

- ✓ Word endings, including adding 's' for a plural and 'ed' for a past tense.

- ✓ Writing in clear sentences, using capital letters and full stops correctly.

Introductory work for many of the above points will be found in the literacy pages in this book.

ALPHABETICAL ORDER

a b c d e f g h i j k l m n o p q r s t u v w x y z

Arrange the foods below into alphabetical order.

Look for the word starting with letter a first.

WORD BOX

chips   milk   banana   fish   yam   grapes   orange
apple   pepper   rice   ham   sugar

1.
2.
3.
4.
5.
6.
7.
8.
9.
10.
11.
12.

Now sort the colour words into alphabetical order.

WORD BOX

red   orange   yellow   green   blue
white   cream   pink   violet   emerald

1.
2.
3.
4.
5.
6.
7.
8.
9.
10.

Colour each square to match the word.

VOWELS AND CONSONANTS

a e i o u = vowels

b c d f g h j k l m n p q r s t v w x y z = consonants

Vowels are very important. They are in most words.

Underline the vowels in the words below:

| school | house | another |

| because | some |

Look at the words again.
Cover them and fill in the missing vowels below.

| sch_ _l | h_ _s_ | _n th_r |

| b_c_ _s_ | s_m_ |

Look at the fish.
Colour all the vowels red.
Colour all the consonants yellow.

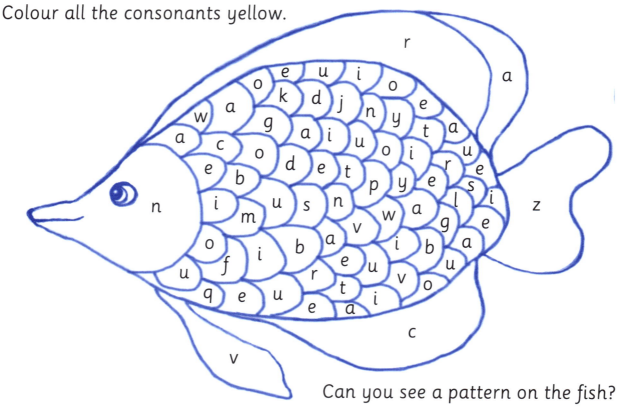

Can you see a pattern on the fish?

ch or ph

Complete the words below by using ph or ch.

| _ _air | _ _ur_ _ | tele_ _one |
| ele_ _ant | mar_ _ | ma_ _ine |

Practise writing 'ch' below.

ch

Practise writing each capital letter.

A B C D E F G
H I J K L M N
O P Q R S T U
V W X Y Z

Copy these words carefully. They each begin with a capital letter.

Monday   Tuesday   Wednesday

Thursday   Friday   Saturday

Sunday

What day is it today?   Today is _____ .

SYLLABLES

Syllables are the 'beats' or 'sounds' that make up a word.

pear = 1 syllable   app le = 2 syllables   ba na na = 3 syllables

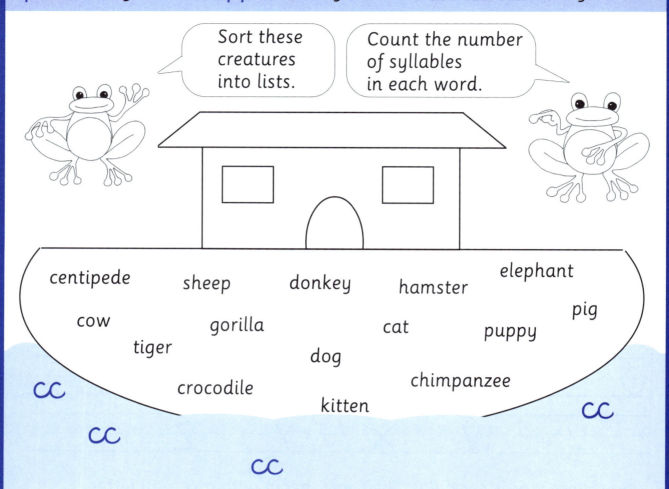

Put each creature in the correct list.

1 syllable	2 syllables	3 syllables

Now complete the water with some more cc shapes.
Use a blue pen or coloured pencil.

Page 4	ODD NUMBERS	1, 3, 5, 7, 9
	EVEN NUMBERS	2, 4, 6, 8, 10
	ODD Shaded Blue	1, 3, 5, 7, 9, 11, 13, 15
	EVEN Shaded Red	2, 4, 6, 8, 10, 12, 14
	MISSING NUMBERS	23, 25, 27, 29, 31, 33, 35
		44, 46, 48, 50, 52, 54, 56, 58
		17, 15, 13, 11, 9

Page 5 ADDITION AND SUBTRACTION

$5 + 1 = 6$, $6 – 5 = 1$
$6 + 2 = 8$, $8 – 6 = 2$
$7 + 3 = 10$, $10 – 7 = 3$
$3 + 2 = 5$, $5 – 3 = 2$
$4 + 2 = 6$, $6 – 4 = 2$
$8 + 5 = 13$, $13 – 8 = 5$
$6 + 6 = 12$, $12 – 6 = 6$
$9 + 7 = 16$, $16 – 9 = 7$
$10 + 10 = 20$, $20 – 10 = 10$

Page 6 CLOCKS
The time is three o'clock.

Page 7 WHAT TIME IS IT?
5 o'clock, half past three, 10 o'clock,
2 o'clock, half past seven, 9 o'clock,
half past one, half past eleven, twelve o'clock/midnight/midday

Page 8 ADDITION STARS
4: $0 + 4, 1 + 3, 2 + 2, 3 + 1, 4 + 0$
5: $0 + 5, 1 + 4, 2 + 3, 3 + 2, 4 + 1, 5 + 0$
6: $0 + 6, 1 + 5, 2 + 4, 3 + 3, 4 + 2, 5 + 1, 6 + 0$

Page 9 7: $0 + 7, 1 + 6, 2 + 5, 3 + 4, 4 + 3, 5 + 2, 6 + 1, 7 + 0$
8: $0 + 8, 1 + 7, 2 + 6, 3 + 5, 4 + 4, 5 + 3, 6 + 2, 7 + 1, 8 + 0$
9: $0 + 9, 1 + 8, 2 + 7, 3 + 6, 4 + 5, 5 + 4, 6 + 3, 7 + 2, 8 + 1, 9 + 0$
10: $0 + 10, 1 + 9, 2 + 8, 3 + 7, 4 + 6, 5 + 5, 6 + 4, 7 + 3, 8 + 2, 9 + 1, 10 + 0$

Page 10 SHAPES
triangle, star, circle, square, rectangle, hexagon, octagon, pentagon

Page 11 NUMBERS IN ORDER OF SIZE
(4, 12, 23)   (5, 17, 48)   (16, 18, 19)   (32, 40, 49)   (6, 15, 43, 58)
(2, 4, 9, 36) (1, 3, 5, 7, 8) (2, 9, 19, 31, 42)

Page 12 THE 2 TIMES TABLE
$2 \times 2 = 4, 3 \times 2 = 6, 4 \times 2 = 8, 5 \times 2 = 10, 6 \times 2 = 12, 7 \times 2 = 14, 8 \times 2 = 16,$
$9 \times 2 = 18, 10 \times 2 = 20$

Page 13 THE 10 TIMES TABLE
$2 \times 10 = 20, 3 \times 10 = 30, 4 \times 10 = 40, 5 \times 10 = 50, 6 \times 10 = 60, 7 \times 10 = 70,$
$8 \times 10 = 80, 9 \times 10 = 90, 10 \times 10 = 100$

Page 14 THE 5 TIMES TABLE
$2 \times 5 = 10, 3 \times 5 = 15, 4 \times 5 = 20, 5 \times 5 = 25, 6 \times 5 = 30, 7 \times 5 = 35, 8 \times 5 = 40,$
$9 \times 5 = 45, 10 \times 5 = 50$

Page 15   HALVING AND DOUBLING
         2 x 3 = 6,   half of 6 = 3
         2 x 5 = 10,   half of 10 = 5
         2 x 7 = 14,   half of 14 = 7
         2 x 6 = 12,   half of 12 = 6
         2 x 10 = 20,   half of 20 = 10

Page 17   ALPHABETICAL ORDER - foods
         1. apple, 2. banana, 3. chips, 4. fish, 5. grapes, 6. ham, 7. milk, 8. orange,
         9. pepper, 10. rice, 11. sugar, 12. yam
         ALPHABETICAL ORDER - colour
         1. blue, 2. cream, 3. emerald, 4. green, 5. orange, 6. pink, 7. red,
         8. violet, 9. white, 10. yellow.

Page 18   VOWELS AND CONSONANTS - underline the vowels
         sch<u>oo</u>l   h<u>ou</u>se   <u>a</u>n<u>o</u>ther   b<u>e</u>c<u>au</u>se   s<u>o</u>m<u>e</u>
         VOWELS AND CONSONANTS - fill in missing vowels
         school   house   another   because   some

         FISH -   Consonants yellow, Vowels red.

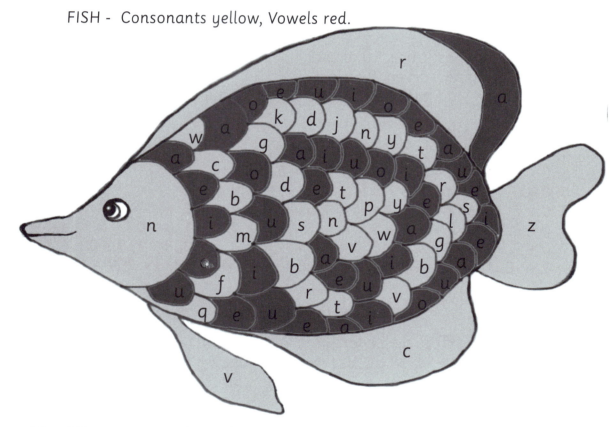

Page 19   CH or PH - put ph or ch in each word.
         chair   church   telephone   elephant   march   machine

Page 20   SYLLABLES - put each creature in the correct list.
         <u>1 syllable.</u>   <u>2 syllables.</u>   <u>3 syllables.</u>
         cow   tiger   gorilla
         dog   kitten   centipede
         pig   puppy   crocodile
         cat   donkey   chimpanzee
         sheep   hamster   elephant

Page 21   COMPOUND WORDS
1. himself, 2. outside, 3. milkman, 4. handbag, 5. airmail, 6. cupboard,
7. pancake, 8. into, 9. teaspoon

Page 22   COMMON WORD ENDINGS - plurals
banana - <u>bananas</u>   cup - <u>cups</u>   house - <u>houses</u>   <u>hand</u> - hands
<u>step</u> - steps   book - <u>books</u>
COMMON WORD ENDINGS - 'ing' and 'ed'
laugh - <u>laughing</u> - <u>laughed</u>   <u>call</u> - <u>calling</u> - called
talk - <u>talking</u> - <u>talked</u>   walk - <u>walking</u> - <u>walked</u>
<u>march</u> - <u>marching</u> - marched   <u>jump</u> - jumping - <u>jumped</u>
push - <u>pushing</u> - <u>pushed</u>

Page 23   WORDS BEGINNING WITH wh
Why can't I go to the party?
When can I have some new shoes?
What are you doing with my books?
Who can I invite to my party?
Which way shall I go?
Where has my kitten gone?

Page 24   UNDERSTANDING TIME IN SENTENCES-Sam's Day
Sam woke up, then went downstairs for breakfast. After breakfast he walked to school. The first lesson was art, Sam's favourite. When art had finished he played with his friends in the playground. It was numeracy from playtime until dinner time. Sam's packed lunch tasted good. After a busy afternoon, Sam walked home. He had tea and at eight o'clock Sam went to bed.

Page 25   SPELLING PATTERNS WITH DIFFERENT SOUNDS - ai
w<u>ai</u>t, <u>air</u>, ch<u>air</u>, r<u>ai</u>n, st<u>air</u>s, f<u>air</u>, tr<u>ai</u>n, m<u>ai</u>n, r<u>ai</u>l
SPELLING PATTERNS WITH DIFFERENT SOUNDS - ea
b<u>ea</u>r, p<u>ea</u>r, <u>ea</u>r, y<u>ea</u>r, f<u>ea</u>r, s<u>ea</u>, <u>ea</u>t, t<u>ea</u>r, <u>ea</u>sy

Page 26   PREFIXES - 'un' or 'dis'
<u>un</u>do, <u>dis</u>appear, <u>dis</u>like, <u>un</u>tidy, <u>dis</u>obey, <u>un</u>zip, <u>dis</u>agree, <u>un</u>lucky, <u>un</u>happy, <u>dis</u>own, <u>un</u>tie, <u>dis</u>honest
SUFFIXES - 'ful' or 'ly'
hope<u>ful</u>, play<u>ful</u>, clear<u>ly</u>, bad<u>ly</u>, week<u>ly</u>, forget<u>ful</u>, pain<u>ful</u>, real<u>ly</u>

Page 27   MISSING WORDS:
1. is, holiday
2. went
3. are, garden
4. am, computer, birthday

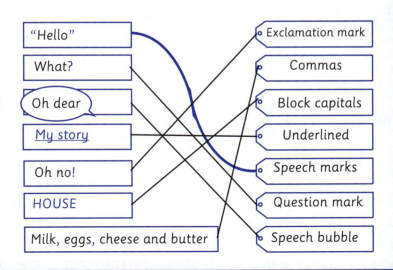

Page 28   ay sound: eight, main, they, sail, may, rain, stay, day
          ee sound: meat, tree, sheep, feet, sea, mean, ski, sweet
          oh sound: blow, toe, goal, hole, snow, soul, stroll, boat
Page 30   FRUIT: apple, banana, strawberries
          VEGETABLE: carrot, peas, potato
Page 31   Three people like apples best.   Two people like bananas best.
          One person likes oranges best.   Four people like strawberries best.

Page 32   Page 33

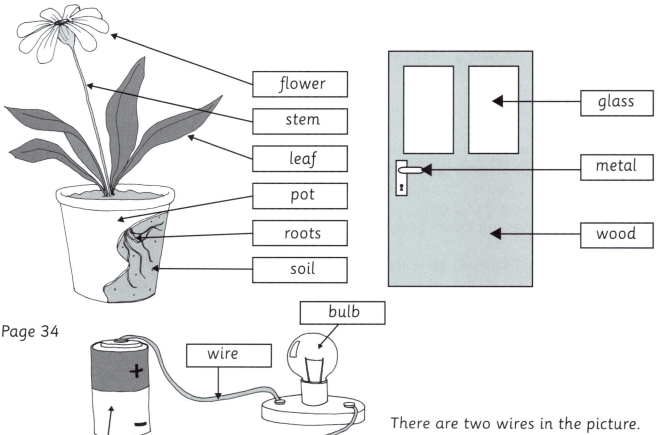

There are two wires in the picture.

Page 37   First picture: Eating ice-creams.
          Second picture: Resting by the car on the journey.
          Third picture: Meeting friends at the swimming pool.
          Fourth picture: Strolling along by the trams on the promenade.

Page 38   First picture: On Sunday September 2nd 1666 a fire started.
          Second picture: The fire spread quickly as the houses were made of wood.
          Third picture: Many people escaped from London by river.
          Fourth picture: After the fire all new houses were made of bricks.

Page 40

COMPOUND WORDS

 "We can put the words *my* and *self* together..."

 "...to make the word *myself*."

Make longer words by putting two short words together.

Beginnings	Endings
him air hand tea in out milk pan cup	bag spoon cake self board to side man mail

1. _____   2. _____   3. _____
4. _____   5. _____   6. _____
7. _____   8. _____   9. _____

Joining letters.
Practise joining *al*, *il* and *wa* below:

il

al

wa

Now write the word wall, on the bricks below.

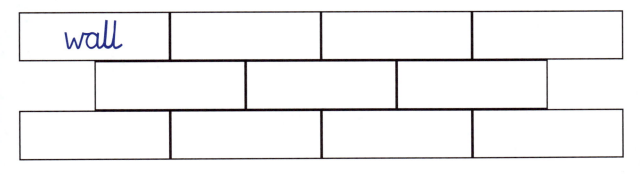

COMMON WORD ENDINGS

 Lots of words add an s when there is more than one.

Complete the chart below:

one	more than one
banana	bananas
cup	_____
house	_____
_____	hands
_____	steps
book	_____

Sometimes we add ing when something is happening now, and ed when something has happened.

e.g.: play   playing   played

Complete this chart:

	ing	ed
laugh	_____	_____
_____	_____	called
_____	talking	_____
walk	_____	_____
_____	_____	marched
_____	jumping	_____
push	_____	_____

22

WORDS BEGINNING WITH wh

These words are often used in questions. They all begin with wh. Practise spelling and writing them below.

	1st try	2nd try
who		
where		
when		
which		
what		
why		

Choose a wh word to begin each question. Remember each sentence begins with a capital letter.

_ _ _ can't I go to the party?

_ _ _ _ can I have some new shoes?

_ _ _ _ _ are you doing with my books?

_ _ _ can I invite to my party?

_ _ _ _ _ way shall I go?

_ _ _ _ _ has my kitten gone?

Practise your best joined writing below.

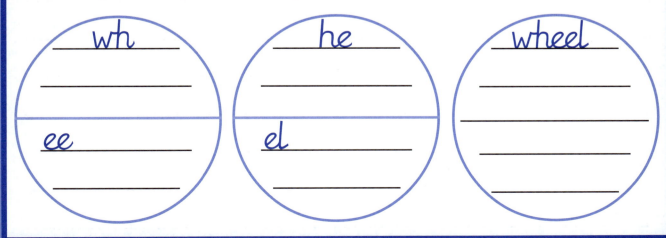

UNDERSTANDING TIME IN SENTENCES

Read these sentences. The numbers show the correct order.

Sam woke up, then went downstairs for breakfast.	1
When art had finished he played with his friends in the playground.	4
After breakfast he walked to school.	2
It was numeracy from playtime until dinner time.	5
He had tea and at eight o'clock Sam went to bed.	8
The first lesson was art, Sam's favourite.	3
Sam's packed lunch tasted good.	6
After a busy afternoon, Sam walked home.	7

Arrange the sentences in the right order below to write the story of Sam's day. Use your best handwriting.

Sam's Day

_____
_____
_____
_____
_____
_____
_____
_____
_____
_____

SPELLING PATTERNS WITH DIFFERENT SOUNDS

Lots of words have ai in them. Practise writing ai below.

ai

Put ai in the words to complete them.

w _ _ t	_ _ r	ch _ _ r
r _ _ n	st _ _ rs	f _ _ r
tr _ _ n	m _ _ n	r _ _ l

Read the words you have made.

Lots of words have ea in them. Practise writing ea below.

ea

Put ea in the words to complete them.

b _ _ r	p _ _ r	_ _ r
y _ _ r	f _ _ r	s _ _
_ _ t	t _ _ r	_ _ sy

25

PREFIXES AND SUFFIXES

Prefixes are at the beginning of words.

un and dis are prefixes. Practise writing them below.

un

dis

Put un or dis before these words to make new words.

_ _ do	_ _ _appear	_ _ _like
_ _ tidy	_ _ _obey	_ _ zip
_ _ _agree	_ _ lucky	_ _ happy
_ _ _own	_ _ tie	_ _ _honest

Can you see that dis and un mean not?

unhappy = not happy   dishonest = not honest

SUFFIXES

Suffixes go at the end of words.

ful and ly are suffixes. Practise writing them.

ful

ly

Put ful or ly after these words.

hope _ _ _	play_ _ _	clear_ _
bad_ _	week_ _	forget_ _ _
pain_ _ _	real_ _	

What do you think ful means?

MISSING WORDS

Put words from the box into the sentences.

WORD BOX

computer   is   garden   are
went   am   birthday   holiday

1. My friend _____ going on _____.
2. The boys _____ out yesterday.
3. The flowers _____ growing in the _____.
4. I _____ hoping to get a new _____ for my _____.

Draw a line to the correct label.

"Hello"	Exclamation mark
What?	Commas
Oh dear (in speech bubble)	Block capitals
My story (underlined)	Underlined
Oh no!	Speech marks
HOUSE	Question mark
Milk, eggs, cheese and butter	Speech bubble

SAME SOUND - DIFFERENT SPELLING

Read these words:

feet	day	sweet	eight	toe	goal	sail	rain
sea	blow	tree	hole	stay	mean	main	boat
soul	they	ski	snow	may	meat	sheep	stroll

Now sort them into groups with the same sound in.

ay sound	ee sound	oh sound

Did you see that different spellings can make the same sound?
Practise your writing in the picture.

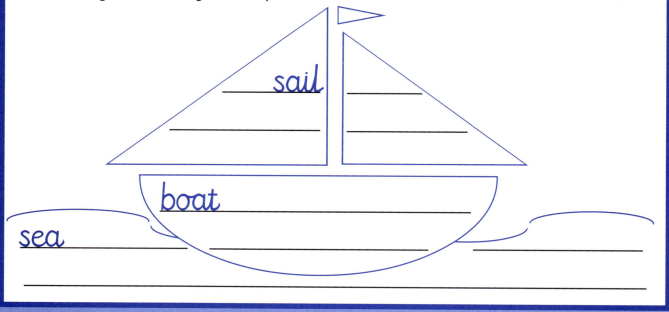

The National Curriculum shows that every child in Year 2 needs to be taught Science and the 'foundation subjects', Art, Design Technology, Geography, History, Information Technology, Music and Physical Education, together with Religious Education.

- ✓ **SCIENCE**
  In Year 2, children will learn about the diet they need to grow healthily. In considering growth, they will learn that humans and other animals reproduce. They will observe plants and animals in the local environment and will need to know the name for parts of plants. They will study materials and how these are changed and used to make other things. They will learn about the forces of pushing and pulling and the effect these forces have on objects.

- ✓ **INFORMATION TECHNOLOGY (IT)**
  Year 2 pupils will use the computer to write sentences. They will use the mouse as a control device when creating pictures. They will find information from a CD-ROM. They will give directions to a floor turtle to control the distance and direction in which it travels.

- ✓ **DESIGN TECHNOLOGY (DT)**
  Children will make observations of vehicles, then design and make their own vehicle with moving wheels. They will examine mechanisms which operate by winding. They may make other products from fabric, e.g. a simple bag or a model of Joseph's coat. They will construct a simple puppet by cutting out and sewing together pieces of fabric. They may use their puppet in their Literacy work.

On the next 5 pages we have included some of the key knowledge and vocabulary that will be of help for your child to Get Ready for Year 2.

FRUIT AND VEGETABLES

Match the words to the pictures.

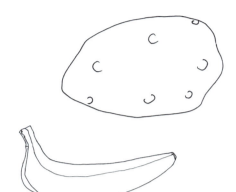

apple

carrot

peas

banana

potato

strawberries

Fruit and vegetables are good for you.

Write each word in the correct list.
Can you think of an extra fruit and an extra vegetable?

FRUIT	VEGETABLE

Which fruit do you like?

Which vegetable do you like?

FRUIT AND VEGETABLES

Ten people chose their favourite fruit.

They made a block chart.

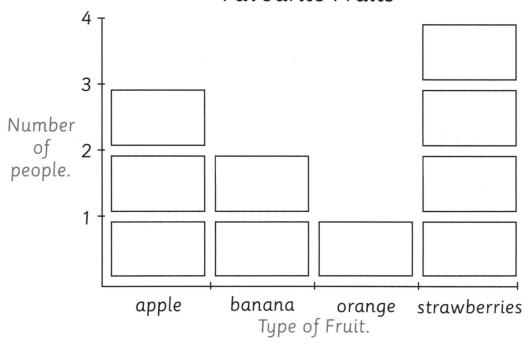

How many people like apples best?

How many people like bananas best?

How many people like oranges best?

How many people like strawberries best?

What is your favourite fruit?

Colour the block chart carefully.

PLANTS

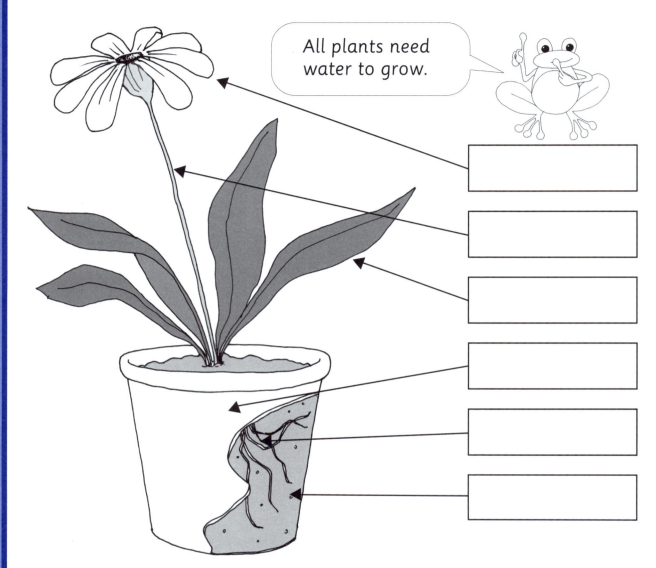

All plants need water to grow.

Label the picture using these words:

roots   pot   leaf   stem   flower   soil

Plant some seeds in a pot.
Water them every day.
Look at them every day.

MATERIALS

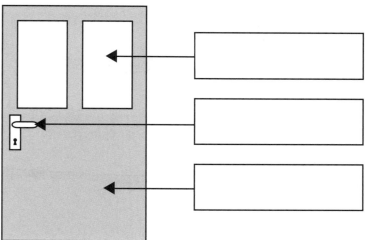

Find something made of wood. What did you find?

Find something made of glass. What did you find?

Find something made of metal. What did you find?

Find something made of plastic. What did you find?

Find something made of cotton. What did you find?

Find something made of paper. What did you find?

ELECTRICITY

Label the picture using these words:
wire   bulb   battery.

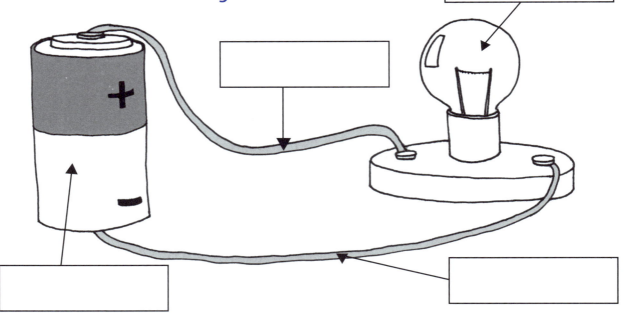

How many wires are in the picture?

Look around you.
Draw something which works by electricity.

What have you drawn?

The National Curriculum shows that every child in Year 2 needs to be taught the 'foundation subjects': Art, Design Technology, Geography, History, Information Technology, Music and Physical Education.
In addition to these subjects, children will be taught Religious Education.

✓ ART
During Year 2, children will draw a self-portrait. They will use a variety of materials for drawing and painting, such as pencils, charcoal, pastels, crayons, block paints, powder paints and liquid paints. They will have opportunities to work with textiles, for example in weaving and collage. They will examine sculptures and produce their own three-dimensional work. They are likely to produce photographs using a digital camera. They will observe the shapes and patterns on buildings.

✓ GEOGRAPHY
In their Year 2 geography work, children will use maps, plans and globes in addition to pictures and photographs. They are likely to learn about an area of this country that is different to their own. They will study the seaside and this work will be linked to their work in history. In looking at maps, globes and atlases they will begin to recognise some places and in particular, they will study one locality overseas which contrasts with the United Kingdom.

✓ HISTORY
In Year 2 children will build upon the historical knowledge and skills developed during Year 1. They may study the Great Fire of London, Florence Nightingale, Remembrance Day and seaside holidays during this year at school.

✓ MUSIC
During Year 2, children build on the musical activities they experienced in Year 1. They will use voices and a range of classroom instruments, perform simple rhythmic and melodic patterns and begin to represent sounds with symbols.

✓ PHYSICAL EDUCATION
In Year 2, children are likely to cover the following aspects of PE:
Dance - the children will create short dances, controlling their body actions to express moods, feelings or other ideas.
Games - the children will be encouraged to work as part of a small team, learning to use space well to avoid their opponents. They will practise basic skills in rolling a ball, as well as kicking it or striking it with a bat.
Gymnastics - the children will improve their control and coordination of balancing, as well as rolling, jumping and landing. They will create simple sequences of balances and movements, sometimes working with a partner.
Swimming - the children will be taught how to float and move in water and how to breathe when swimming.

In all P.E. activities the children will take part in warming up and cooling down activities and will learn of the effects that exercise has on the body.

✓ RELIGIOUS EDUCATION
During Year 2, children are likely to study: religious celebrations, the importance of the Torah to Jewish people, why Jesus told stories, and they may have the opportunity to visit a place of worship. The activity page in this book introduces vocabulary they may encounter during the year.

GEOGRAPHY

Some people send postcards to their friends when they go on holiday.
Draw a picture on this postcard. The picture could be of the seaside on your holiday.

Now write a message to your friends.
Tell them about the seaside.

Draw the stamp.

Address:

HISTORY – HOLIDAYS AT THE SEASIDE 70 YEARS AGO

Write the correct sentence for each picture.

1. Meeting friends at the swimming pool.
2. Eating ice-creams.
3. Strolling along by the trams on the promenade.
4. Resting by the car on the journey.

THE FIRE OF LONDON

Write the correct sentence under each picture to tell the story of the Fire of London. Then colour the pictures.

Many people escaped from London by river.

On Sunday 2nd September 1666, a fire started.

After the fire all new houses were made of bricks.

The fire spread quickly as the houses were made of wood.

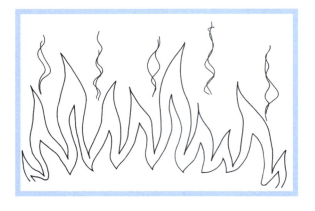

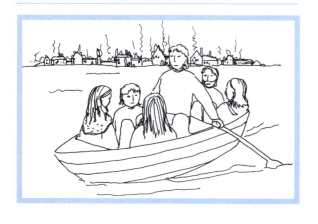

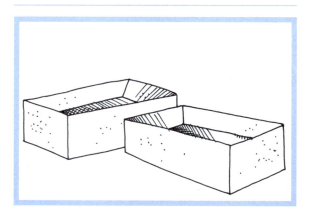

MUSICAL SOUNDS

Gentle music on the xylophone makes me think of sunny days.

Fast beats on the triangle make me think of windy days.

What do you think?
Join each weather picture to an instrument.

rain

xylophone

thunderstorm

maracas

wind

triangle

sun

cymbals
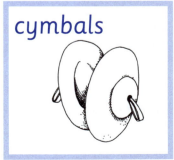

RELIGIOUS CELEBRATIONS

Look at the words in the boxes.

They are all about religious celebrations.

JEWISH	CHRISTIAN	HINDU
Pesach Hanukkah	Christmas Easter	Diwali Holi

Can you find these six words in the word search below?
You can draw rings like this:

… or this:

p	e	s	a	c	h	j	t	e	c	i	s	z
w	a	t	l	o	h	a	n	u	k	k	a	h
q	s	b	f	d	i	w	a	l	i	y	n	m
e	t	v	g	h	t	x	p	h	o	l	i	r
d	e	b	u	w	q	c	h	f	l	k	w	m
v	r	x	y	c	h	r	i	s	t	m	a	s

Practise spelling the names of these religions:

Islam	Buddhism	Sikhism